Fear factor

THE FRIGHT STUFF!

By Jesse Leon McCann

SCHOLASTIC INC.

New York   Toronto   London   Auckland   Sydney

Mexico City   New Delhi   Hong Kong   Buenos Aires

■ SCHOLASTIC

All *Fear Factor* stunts are designed and supervised by trained professionals.
They are extremely dangerous and should not be attempted by anyone, anywhere, anytime!

ISBN 0-439-79049-2

™ & © 2005 Endemol Netherlands B.V.

Published by Scholastic Inc.
SCHOLASTIC and associated logos are trademarks and/or registered trademarks of Scholastic Inc.

12 11 10 9 8 7 6 5 4 3 2 1   5 6 7 8 9/0

Designed by Michelle Martinez Design, Inc.
Printed in the U.S.A.
First printing, September 2005

Introduction

When Does Fear Become a Factor for You?

Is it a slither in the **SHADOWS**? A bump in the **NIGHT**? A glance over the **EDGE** of a one-hundred-foot **DROP**? Is it an **EXPLOSION**? The sound of deep, **CHURNING** water? The skitter of tiny **CLAWS** across your bedroom floor?

When does **FEAR** become a **FACTOR** for you?

On the hit TV show *Fear Factor*, that's what contestants aim to find out for themselves in every episode.

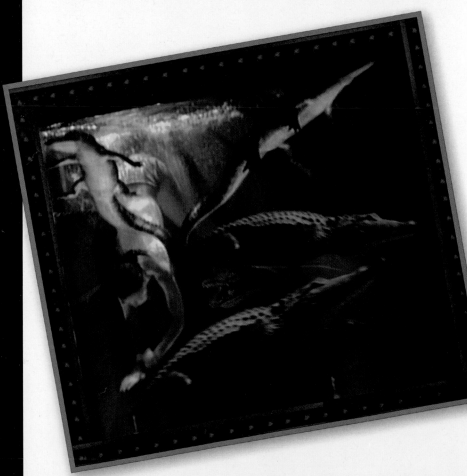

For its millions of viewers, *Fear Factor* generates thrills, spills, and creepy chills! **WHY?** Because fans have discovered that watching people **FACE THEIR FEARS** can be fun!

Resistance is futile. *Fear Factor*, which began its life as little more than a gross-out blip on the TV screen—and wasn't expected to survive longer than a season or two—is now a certified hit, going into its sixth season. That's more than 120 hours of stunts so awesome, viewers can't take their eyes off the screen, even as their stomachs are turning.

No doubt about it, *Fear Factor* is huge! As a phenomenon, it has spawned every kind of merchandise, from T-shirts to tea mugs, even night-lights. Who wouldn't be afraid of the dark after watching a creepy-crawly episode?

There's even a brand-new *Fear Factor* ride at the Universal Studios theme parks in Florida and California. Are you ready to strap yourself in? The pictures and 411 on the following pages are going to be bumpy!

FEAR FACT

Rejected *Fear Factor* show titles:

- Addicted to Danger

- Scared Stiff

- Survive This...

- On the Edge

When you watch *Fear Factor*, do you ask yourself if you'd be too chicken to perform the stunts? Do you break into a cold sweat at the thought of hanging from a helicopter? Would you pass out if you found a snake on your shoulder? Would you squirm if you had to eat something really yucky?

In this book, we'll revisit some of the greatest stunts on *Fear Factor*, highlight some of the records that contestants have set, hear what players experienced in their own words, and test your *Fear Factor* knowledge. We'll even explore some weird phobias that people have. For example, did you know some people have ablutophobia? That's the fear of taking a bath!

Of course, we'll also show you people eating and being covered in really gross stuff! So, sit back and enjoy the ride. And remember: All *Fear Factor* stunts are designed and supervised by trained professionals. They are extremely dangerous and should not be attempted by anyone, anywhere, anytime!

FEAR FACT

Fear Factor medical help is always just one bloodcurdling scream away.

CHAPTER 1

FAST & FURIOUS!

Planes, trains, and automobiles. Tractor trailers, helicopters, dune buggies, and Jet Skis. When there's a need for scary speed on powerful machines, *Fear Factor* delivers!

Who can forget when the monster truck crushed the contestant's car before he could drive away? Or when players had to jump from one speeding boat to another? Or the time they had to walk on the wing of a biplane at 4,000 feet in the air? Well, there are probably a few contestants who'd like to forget!

STARTLING STATISTICS!

Fear Factor Vehicle Records

Fastest time driving a car up a ramp and onto the bed of a moving semitruck while blindfolded: 12 seconds.

Fastest time by a team of two dropping from a helicopter onto a floating target of boxes, retrieving a flag, and swimming it to a nearby platform: 1 minute, 44 seconds.

Fastest time passing flags from one speeding eighteen-wheeler to another while balanced between them: 1 minute, 9 seconds.

Contestants in this challenge have to find the key that will start the car and drive to the finish line. Easy, right?

But what if there's a monster truck heading for you? This contestant better get out of the way!

A Different Kind of Drag Race!

Ah, the covered wagon, a simple vehicle from the olden days! Not the most comfortable way to travel, though. Especially when you're getting dragged behind it, and have to climb a cargo net into the back of a speeding wagon!

Talk about eating somebody's dust! (And gravel and rocks, too!)

Of course, we know that *Fear Factor* contestants have to eat lots worse things than that! (More about that in the next chapter.)

WAGON GAMES

Pioneer children played lots of games on the long journey west, like jumping rope, chasing wooden hoops, and tag. But dragging was something they never would have thought of. Pioneers walked beside their covered wagons to lighten the load for the horses and oxen.

CONTESTANT Q&A

Question: What was the most daring and dangerous thing you did before appearing on *Fear Factor*?

Contestants' Answers:
"I went to Spain . . . and believe it or not, I ran with the bulls!"
"I got locked on a rooftop and had to jump to a fire escape."
"Riding my motorcycle at a speed of 140 miles per hour."
"I climbed down a rock face sixty feet."
"Cliff diving off ledges into lakes. Who knows what you're gonna hit?"
"Went skydiving on my twenty-seventh birthday."
"Penning cows. We had a herd of eighty cows, and we had to round them up in a little pen. Let's just say they weren't very happy, so they would kick and buck and I had to be in there with them."

9

It can be hard enough to drive on the highway, but halfway onto the back of a moving truck? Forget about it! These players had to drive two wheels only onto the flatbed truck and knock down flags along the way. Then they had to do the same thing on the other side.

Fear Factor contestants often get the chance to drive through things, an activity usually reserved for movie stunt drivers! These players launched themselves off a ramp, through a house, and out a stained-glass window. The winner "flew" a distance of 29 feet, 11.5 inches.

Not the easiest way to change rides—but at 40 miles per hour, the quickest! Players jumped from moving dump truck to moving dump truck, transferring flags from one to the other.

Of course, trained *Fear Factor* personnel are always on hand to make sure contestants are safely attired in case they get hung out to dry!

A Race to Drive the Players Buggy!

BUGGY FEVER

Dune buggies are a fast and furious way to race across the desert. U.S. Special Forces modified dune buggies to create the Desert Patrol Vehicle for use in the Middle East. DPVs are almost impossible to catch, racing ahead of other U.S. troops to scout territory and dart behind enemy lines. They get in, do the job, and get out—fast. Talk about fearless!

Phobia Puzzler

What are people with Barophobia afraid of?

   A. Metal bars
   B. Barometers
   C. Gravity
   D. Speeding vehicles

Answer: c. The fear of gravity.

On *Fear Factor*, dune buggies can be a real drag! These players were dragged by their ankles as the buggies raced across the beach. But that's not all — they had to hold on to their partners with a piece of rope.

Could you hold on, or would your partner leave you in the dust?

Come Fly with Us!

Nothing can match the raw nerve it takes to strap yourself into a car, flip that hurling mass of metal on a ramp at a high rate of speed, and land sliding and smashing onto the pavement. Some call that fearless. Others call it crazy!

Here's a *Fear Factor* challenge you'll flip for!

Wheeeee! The winner launched his car 92 feet, 4 inches.

Contestants had to race their cars head-on into another car with a pipe ramp. They had to hit the moving ramp at exactly the right spot to flip their cars. This driver *ramped* it up!

CRASH!

French inventor Nicholas-Joseph Cugnot had the first motor vehicle accident in 1771. He drove his steam-powered tricycle into a stone wall. Cugnot designed the first automobile in 1769. His steam-powered, three-wheeled military tractor carried four people and was used by the French Army to haul artillery at a whopping speed of two and half miles per hour. It had to stop every 10 to 20 minutes to build up steam power.

Fear Factor players have driven cars over trucks, under trucks, onto trucks, over the roofs of other cars, and even into pools. More than 75 cars were wrecked in the first five seasons.

CHAPTER 2 The Taste of Fear!

When we were little kids, we sometimes ate **DEAD BUGS** and dog biscuits on a dare. Now we might chow down on **THREE-DAY-OLD** hot dogs from the mini-mart, or **COLD PIZZA** for breakfast. So it shouldn't be that **FRIGHTENING** to eat some of the dishes they serve on *Fear Factor*, should it? Oh, but it is!

How about we start with a nice fish dinner? This challenge is called... COD STEW!

This is a self-serve meal. The player reaches inside the dead cod and pulls out the chip that will tell him what's for dinner.

Yummy! Cod egg sack, cod liver, and other cod parts. It's the combo plate! Mmm... fish parts.

How is everything? Don't tell us— your expression speaks volumes!

FEAR FACT

Codfish can weigh as much as 200 pounds. These hungry predators eat herring, sand eel, and other fishes.

Dude, that's disgusting!

We asked a *Fear Factor* contestant her strategy for squeezing the liquid from a cow's eyeball into a cup with her mouth. "Get a good grip on it with your teeth and pop it. The juices would fly in the back of your throat and outside the cup, so it was hard to get the juices right in the cup. A lot of it was going down your throat, all in your mouth, so that part was definitely gross. It tasted kinda salty, like dirt water."

Cow brains are not the only kind served on *Fear Factor*. Players have also chowed down on pig and sheep brains.

The Players Who Ate Brains from Another Creature!

Brains are considered gourmet food in some countries, whether they're fried, baked, or broiled— but not the way they're served on *Fear Factor*. Gross doesn't even begin to describe it.

Some people believe if you eat another animal's brain, you'll gain their intelligence. Wonder if this contestant started mooing and eating grass?

Is the taste of the brains causing her to make that face, or the stinky cow spinal fluid?

DUE: Noun / 1: a preparation melted cheese.

Introducing *Fear Factor* fondue! We found the stinkiest, moldiest, foulest-smelling cheese on the planet. Then we melted it into a warm, creamy glop.

The players had to stick their heads in . . .

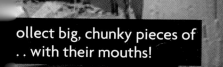

ollect big, chunky pieces of . . with their mouths!

FEAR FACTS:

Bugs for Dinner

- Giant horse grasshoppers, also known as horse lubber grasshoppers, are 1.5 to 2.5 inches long, with six legs, four wings, and two antennae.

- People around the world eat more than 1,500 different species of insects. In South America, movie theaters sell roasted ants. Markets in Thailand sell grasshoppers and water bugs to eat.

- The average person eats about one pound of insects each year by accident. How many creepy-crawlies have you swallowed?

The fondue challenge is topped off by eating five live giant horse grasshoppers! Yum, yum! You can feel their legs still moving as they go down!

Watch it, dude! She might hurl!

Bleahh! She ate them.

A *Fear Factor* Power Breakfast?
EGG-ZACTLY!

Did you know ostrich eggs are the world's largest egg? They're six inches around and contain three pounds of yolk and membrane—that's as much as 24 chicken eggs. You have to break them open with a hammer. What a great way to start the day: swallowing a raw ostrich egg!

Don't worry, Johnny.
There's no one
watching.
(Or is there?)

Interview with an Ostrich Egg Eater:

Contestant **Summer Papania**

FEAR FACTOR: So, how was it?
SUMMER PAPANIA: It smelled horrible, and it tasted even more horrible, and it felt even more horrible than that.

FEAR FACTOR: Compare it to other gross things you've eaten before.
SUMMER PAPANIA: That's the grossest thing I've ever eaten, honestly.

FEAR FACTOR: At first, it looked like you'd never get through it.
SUMMER PAPANIA: I gave up and psyched myself out after the first two sips, and I think that's what made it worse for me. I said, "I can't do this, there's no way." And then, I just kept doing it, and I kept gagging.

FEAR FACTOR: Do you normally eat eggs?
SUMMER PAPANIA: No. I can't stand eggs.

FEAR FACTOR: Did it make it worse for you when your opponents started trash-talking?
SUMMER PAPANIA: Yes. I was already feeling really negative and feeling really down about it—so much so that I wanted to cry. They were talking about how bad it tasted.

FEAR FACTOR: So they were making it seem worse than it was?
SUMMER PAPANIA: Oh, no, they were being honest—it tasted BAD. But they didn't have to tell me. I already knew that.

FEAR FACTOR: How did this experience compare with other struggles in your life?
SUMMER PAPANIA: I'm telling you, this is the worst thing I've ever done.

FEAR FACTOR: Do you think this will have a lasting effect on you?
SUMMER PAPANIA: Probably forever. I'm never eating another egg again. I'm not even looking at ostriches.

C'mon! That was only your first sip! Take a big gulp.

That's more like it! Now, keep it all in.

Uh-oh! You lost a strand!

FEARSOME FACTS

- The ostrich is the largest and heaviest bird in the world. It can grow up to nine feet tall and weigh as much as 345 pounds.

- Ostriches can't fly, but they can run faster than any other bird—up to 43 miles per hour.

- The ostrich has the biggest eyeballs of any bird. They are two inches across.

- Ostriches don't really bury their heads in the sand. When they're threatened, ostriches lay their heads against the sand to try and blend in with it.

Fear Factor Goes Italian!

Start with bile-based crust. Pour on some cow-blood sauce. Add some stinky cheese, and top it all off with fish eyes and live worms. *Voilà! Fear Factor* pizza!

What was it like to eat a slice of *Fear Factor* pizza?

Contestant: "I put the first bite in my mouth. But as soon as I tried to get the first bite down and actually swallow, it was just over from that point. Not being able to get the first bite down without gagging totally made me say to myself, 'I don't know if I can do this.' I really started doubting myself after that first bite."

EXTRA! EXTRA!

Joe Rogan Eats Sheep Eyes. Every stunt is tested and re-tested to make sure the contestants don't get *too* sick. *Fear Factor* host Joe Rogan even ate sheep eyes to see what the players had to face.

There's nothing more moving than a well-made pizza pie. But in this case, it's the pizza that's moving!

He'd better hope the worms don't crawl up his nose.

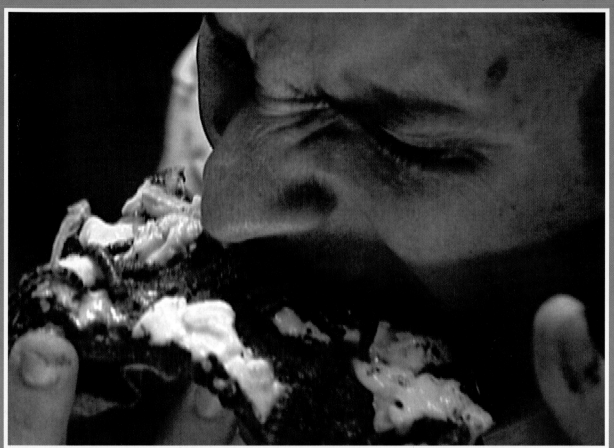

There's also spaghetti and meatballs—
Fear Factor style, of course!

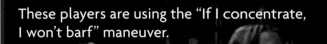

These players are using the "If I concentrate, I won't barf" maneuver.

"Think happy thoughts! Think happy thoughts!"

LET'S EAT! Special of the Day!

Our soup of the day is a succulent fish sauce!

FEAR FACTOR FOOD RULES

Rule One: You can never have enough brains. Brains are gross.

Rule Two: You can never have enough pig parts.

Rule Three: Add in as many stinky ingredients as you can.

Our entrée is intestines . . .

LET'S EAT!

Special of the Day!

WORMS!

In just five seasons, *Fear Factor* contestants have eaten or drunk more than a thousand worms, including:

- Red Worms
- Super Worms
- Night Crawlers
- Mealworms
- Wax Worms
- Tomato Hornworms
- Silkworms
- And that doesn't even include the maggots!

. . . with a side order of worms . . .

. . . and more worms!

HEY, you've got something in your teeth!

CONTESTANT QUIZ!

Q: What do most contestants say is the grossest part of the "Gross Food" stunts?

   a. The look
   b. The taste
   c. The smell

Answer: c. The smell! Aren't you glad there's no such thing as Stench–O–Vision?!

The TEN Grossest

Things *Fear Factor* Contestants Consumed!

- **Maggot-and-House-Fly Shake**
- Ant-covered Cod Egg Sacks
- *Fear Factor* **Pizza**
- African Cave-Dwelling Spiders
- **Tomato Hornworms**
- Madagascar Hissing Cockroaches
- **Cow Eyeballs**
- Rat Stew
- **Spaghetti Made of Worms and Coagulated Blood**
- Blended Banana Slugs

World's Most Dangerous Fruit

Fear Factor's foulest–smelling recipes often include fruit from the durian tree. Durian is known as the world's most dangerous fruit. Its egg–shaped rind is covered with hard, sharp spines. A human hit by a falling durian can be seriously injured or even killed. The fruit's pulp smells so bad that it's been banned in public places in Southeast Asia, where the tree grows.

CHAPTER 3

All Creatures Great and Slimy!

Fear Factor contestants garner an excellent opportunity to get up close and personal with all sorts of critters. From slugs, spiders, and leeches, to rats, sharks, and gators, our intrepid contenders go head to head in every episode. And for their dedication, we say . . . let 'em! We'll stay home where it's safe!

Shocks and Squeals
When You Play with Eels!

That's 1,000 volts of pure electric eels there. Players had to transfer six eels from one side of the tank to the other, using one hand so they didn't get shocked to death!

They seem harmless, right? Riiiiiight!

Are you sure you want to get so close? It looks dangerous!

THE SHOCKING TRUTH!

Connecting with a Player on Electric Eels:

"I knew I was gonna get shocked, but once I got up there and I went to grab the eel, I felt like I couldn't let go of it. And it just kept shocking and shocking and shocking. You almost can't pull away from it. The more I grabbed, the more it just shocked my body. It was weird!"

FEARSOME FACTS!

- Electric eels aren't true eels. They are fish with an eel–like shape.

- Electric eels can produce electric currents as high as 650 volts. Your computer runs on just 120 volts.

- Electric eels don't have teeth—they shock their prey, usually a smaller fish, and then swallow it whole.

29

Another Challenge, Different Eels!

These are moray eels. Their razor-sharp teeth hurt like crazy. Our competitors had to move them out of the way to gather keys from the bottom of the tank—and they had to do it while hanging upside-down by their ankles!

"My, what big teeth you have!"

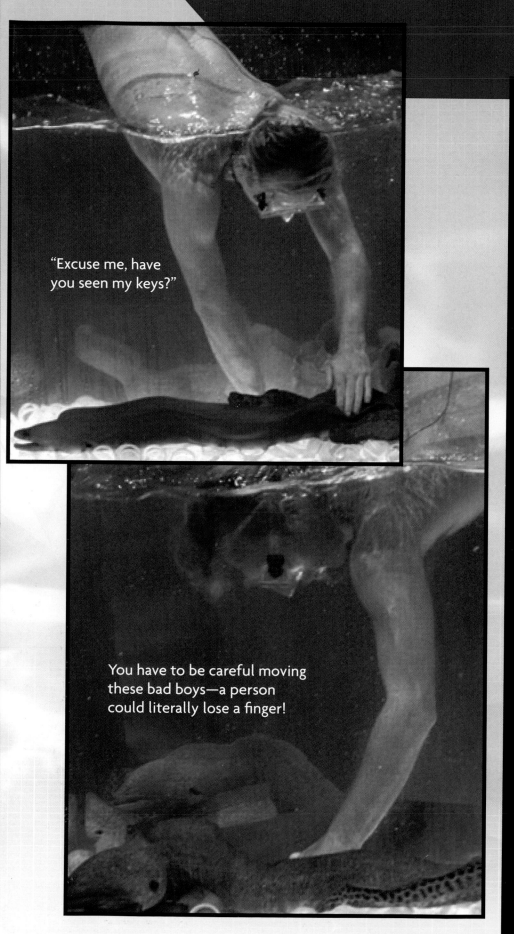

"Excuse me, have you seen my keys?"

You have to be careful moving these bad boys—a person could literally lose a finger!

➤ Moray eels have strong, razor-sharp teeth that enable them to seize their prey and to inflict serious injury on their enemies.

➤ Moray eels have double-hinged jaws. They can eat prey several times the size of their own heads.

➤ Moray eels are the top predator in the underwater reefs where they live.

A Real Eel Trivia Quiz!

Q: What do moray eels primarily eat?
   a. Seaweed
   b. Crustaceans
   c. Fish eggs

Answer: b. You know it! Moray eels munch on crustaceans like shrimp, crab, and sea urchin.

Q: How would you describe the personality of moray eels?
   a. Aggressive
   b. Shy
   c. Outgoing and social

Answer: b. Moray eels are actually very shy. Except when they're hunting, of course.

Q: The electric eel's shock-producing organs are located . . .
   a. in its tail
   b. on its head
   c. on its tongue

Answer: a. These cells are concentrated in the electric eel's tail, which occupies four-fifths of the total length of the fish. Electric eels can grow to lengths of six to nine feet.

FROM THE OLD-JOKES ARCHIVE

Q: How do you make a rat shake?

A: Tell him a scary story!

Ratty Trivia Quiz!

Q: Which of the following are rats unable to do?
   a. Hold their breath for 3 minutes
   b. Gnaw through lead
   c. Crawl through a .25-inch hole

Answer: c. Rats need at least a .5-inch opening to invade your space!

Q: How long can a rat tread water?
   a. 1 minute
   b. 6 hours
   c. 3 days

Answer: c. Yikes! Rats can paddle for up to three days!

Q: Which rat fact is true?
   a. Rats have 43 bones.
   b. Rats have belly buttons.
   c. Rats have thumbs.

Answer: b. Rats do have belly buttons. Cute!

Aw, Rats!

Rats are extremely intelligent. Too intelligent to go people bobbing. This challenge had the ladies lying in a tank with more than 400 live rats, while their partners used their mouths to retrieve ten hidden chicken feet. It isn't easy staying calm as rats crawl up and down your body, clawing and biting along the way!

Which is worse—having to stick your face into a tank full of rats, or . . . wait—there's nothing worse than sticking your face into a tank full of rats.

"Pardon me, sir. I really must compliment you on your fine, luxurious beard!"

RAT ~~ATTACK!~~

Fear Factor animal wranglers are always stressed out when rats are involved in a challenge. Rats are unpredictable. No matter how many precautions the handlers take, there's always a chance that rats will attack.

"Oh, sorry, miss. My mistake!"

What's the Buzz?

Fear Factor is all about facing your fears. But what happens when conquering those fears means facing hundreds of thousands of bees? In this challenge, bees swarmed one twin while the other searched for keys that would set his or her sibling free.

While this contestant was covered in thousands of bees and shackled between two poles, her twin sister had to search through a bee-filled stack of drawers to find the keys that would set her sister loose. By the end of the challenge, each sister had been stung over thirty times!

Notice this player's relaxed, meditative state. *Some people can sleep anywhere!*

It's the latest fashion—matching bee caps and sweaters.

FEARSOME FACTS!

- Bees' wings beat more than 11,000 cycles per minute.

- Bees have five eyes—three simple eyes that distinguish between light and dark, and two complex eyes that detect movement.

- When the honeybee stings, it leaves behind its stinger and venom pouch in your skin and soon dies.

- Bees don't create honey. Honey is plant nectar that bees have regurgitated (yup, thrown up) and dehydrated.

FEAR FACT

Fear Factor hires professional animal handlers that raise and take care of the animals used on the show. When animals are involved in a challenge, the handlers make sure the contestants and the animals are kept safe. Usually that means making sure the animals are well fed before a stunt, so the players don't get eaten for dinner.

Snakes Alive!

So they slither, and have scales, and they never close their eyes. What's a snake or two between friends? Here's a list of snakes *Fear Factor* players have had to face head—on:

- Mandarin Rat Snakes
- Asian Rat Snakes
- Tiger Rat Snakes
- Rough Green Snakes
- Amazon Tree Boas
- Red Tail Boas
- Ball Pythons
- Corn Snakes
- Albino Corn Snakes
- Anerthirstic Corn Snakes
- Hypo Corn Snakes
- Snow Corn Snakes
- Ribbon Snakes
- Northern Garter Snakes
- Canadian Garter Snakes

Fear of snakes, or ophidiophobia, is the number-one phobia. Acrophobia, or fear of heights, is number two. If you had bibliophobia—fear of books—you wouldn't be reading this.

Ablutophobia is the fear of taking a bath. Ophidiophobia is the fear of snakes. Put them together, and you have the next challenge. Players had to find three keys in a bathtub filled with a hundred snakes!

Players' hands and feet were handcuffed. Only those keys would set them free.

What's scarier, swimming with snakes or taking the walk of shame?

The Grumbling Gator Challenge!

Participants had to perform tasks in a cold, murky swamp for this challenge, searching for keys.

The first key was in the water, and the second key was in the rowboat. The third was up a tree—just don't fall on top of McNasty. To get to the fourth key, players had to haul McNasty the alligator out of a sewer pipe—by his tail.

McNasty got his name for a reason—this is one cranky alligator.

A *Fear Factor* Favorite: Madagascar Hissing Cockroaches!

Add one boy . . .

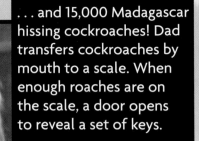

. . . and 15,000 Madagascar hissing cockroaches! Dad transfers cockroaches by mouth to a scale. When enough roaches are on the scale, a door opens to reveal a set of keys.

He's got the keys. Now, which one will unlock him?

"Keys! I need the keys!"

Here comes Mom with the keys and words of wisdom.

Not a happy camper.

She concentrates on her task: Escape!

- Madagascar hissing cockroaches are two inches long and have spindly legs and two antennae that never stop moving.

- 15,000 Madagascar hissing cockroaches weigh approximately 470 pounds.

- The Madagascar hissing cockroach lives for two to five years.

- To keep the cockroaches in the coffin, the rim is coated with petroleum jelly.

- Male roaches sometimes battle each other for as long as half an hour, hissing twenty to thirty times.

How Do They Do That?

- Native tribes in South America use the piranha's razor-sharp teeth to make tools and weapons.

- Piranha can grow to as long as two feet and swim in large schools.

- The red-bellied piranha's razor-sharp teeth can shred flesh from bone in seconds.

FEARSOME FACTS!

- Ancient scorpions lived before dinosaurs and were three to four feet long.

- Scorpions paralyze their prey with a stinger at the end of their tails.

- Scorpions can live without food for up to one year, and underwater for two days.

How could *Fear Factor* contestants possibly swim in a tank of flesh-eating piranhas and live to tell about it? The ferocious fish were fed to the gills with pig's kidneys before the stunt. The piranhas were too full to eat anymore . . . or so we hoped!

What in the world are *Fear Factor* contestants thinking, getting into a pit with thousands of live scorpions? *Fear Factor* has professional medical staff standing by for every stunt. If a player were to have a life-threatening number of scorpion stings, the medics would go into action. And, of course, a doctor examines the contestants after every stunt.

Still, that's little consolation when the creepy-crawlies are scampering all over you!

CHAPTER 4

Hang in There, Baby!

You can conquer your fear of bugs, eating gross foods, and racing high-speed vehicles. But if you don't master your fear of heights, *Fear Factor* will pick you up and drop you down! Blue skies aren't so sunny when there's a hundred feet of nothing between you and Mother Earth!

These contestants had to traverse a swaying beam, high over the water.

BUCKLE UP FOR SAFETY

Safety gear worn by *Fear Factor* contestants includes goggles, helmets, mouth guards (to keep players from biting off their tongues!), body armor, fire-retardant suits, and life vests, depending on the challenge.

In insect challenges, goggles and earplugs make sure those creepy-crawlies can't bite eyes or tunnel their way into players' heads. Ewwww!

Oops! As always, this *Fear Factor* contestant wore protective gear . . .

. . . so he wouldn't be left hanging.

Ever Wonder What Your Laundry Feels Like?

Two tumblers like this one were side by side, up in the air, high above the ocean. As the tumblers turned, players had to capture flags, pass them to each other, and place them on the other end. The problem? These tumblers had big holes.

To make things more interesting, the rotation of the tumblers sped up over time.

Watch out for the holes! Hit the water and you're going home.

Take it one step at a time. But hurry, hurry, hurry.

Mini Pocket Bike Challenge!

otorized mini pocket bikes rule! But when the players had to ride one across a narrow beam between two platforms, suspended more than a hundred feet above the ground, they wondered if they were riding their pint-size, powerful motorcycles to their doom!

Fear factor PHOBIA QUIZ

You've heard of arachnophobia (fear of spiders) and claustrophobia (fear of confined spaces), but can you match these phobia names with their fears?

1. Testophobia
2. Phasmophobia
3. Taphophobia
4. Myxophobia
5. Achluophobia
6. Lachanophobia
7. Arachibutyrophobia
8. Herpetophobia
9. Triskadekaphobia
10. Coulrophobia

a. Fear of cemeteries
b. Fear of creepy-crawly things
c. Fear of the dark
d. Fear of taking tests
e. Fear of number thirteen
f. Fear of vegetables
g. Fear of ghosts
h. Fear of clowns
i. Fear of peanut butter sticking to the roof of your mouth
j. Fear of slime

Answers: 1–d, 2–g, 3–a, 4–j, 5–c, 6–f, 7–i, 8–b, 9–e, 10–h

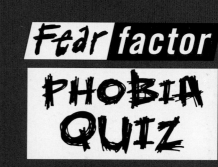

Let's Not Forget the Unsung Stars of *Fear Factor* – the Helicopters!

Jumping, hanging, and climbing stunts are more exciting (and a lot more difficult) when helicopters are involved. Here's a page dedicated to the helicopters, the unofficial stars of *Fear Factor*!

STARTLING HELICOPTER STATISTICS!

Best time climbing up a ladder and into a chopper as the helicopter spun above the cold Pacific Ocean: **1 minute, 1 second.**

Fastest time climbing out of one side of a helicopter, traversing underneath it using a cargo net, and climbing in the other side: **40 seconds.**

Most flags gathered from buoys while hanging upside-down from a helicopter as it flew past the buoys spaced twenty feet apart: **15 flags.**

Best time and most flags transferred by a player crossing back and forth on a swaying beam lifted by two helicopters: **4 flags in 1 minute, 55.6 seconds.**

Look at that whirlybird fly! Looks fun, right? But what if you had to drop out of one, into the water?

In this stunt, players had to hold on for as long as they could until the chopper hovered over a target zone. Hold on, or fall into a freezing lake below! Dropping from a helicopter into a lake was just the beginning in this challenge. Players then had to swim to a raft and make it to shore—in the wake created by the chopper's blades.

Viva Las Vegas!

One of the most dynamic stunts ever seen on *Fear Factor* involved contestants sliding down one side of a Las Vegas glass pyramid hotel, the Luxor, and grabbing flags along the way.

After climbing out a window on the twenty-ninth floor, near the pointy top of the pyramid, players slid down the side of the hotel between two rows of *Fear Factor* flags.

"Honey, I think someone just slid past our hotel window!"

Gathering flags at that speed at night, with bright lights shining in their faces, was a daunting task for the players. The winner snagged eight flags.

ANCIENT EGYPT IN AMERICA

🗨 The Luxor Hotel in Las Vegas is named after Luxor, Egypt—the site of some of ancient Egypt's most famous temples and tombs.

🗨 The hotel's ten–story sphinx is taller than the original and was built more than four thousand years later. But like the original Great Sphinx of Giza, near the Egyptian pyramids, it has the body of a lion and the head of a king, with an opening in its left paw. The original is about 66 feet high and 240 feet long.

Players wore special non-friction suits and traveled at a speed of twenty-five feet per minute.

Fear of heights is one of the most common phobias. Maybe that's why *Fear Factor* dreamed up these challenges:

- Climbing down a 35–foot ladder on a blimp hovering 1,000 feet above the ocean.

- Releasing flags from the pontoons of a float plane as it flew up to 2,000 feet above a lake.

- Walking on the wing of a moving biplane flying at a 100 miles per hour, three thousand feet above Earth.

The Most Dangerous Gamble in Las Vegas

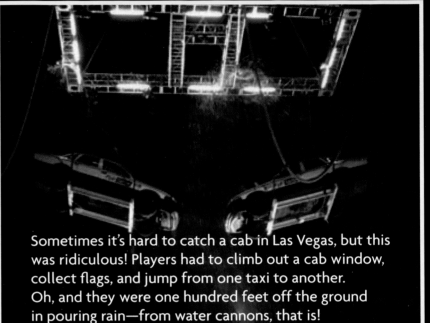

Sometimes it's hard to catch a cab in Las Vegas, but this was ridiculous! Players had to climb out a cab window, collect flags, and jump from one taxi to another. Oh, and they were one hundred feet off the ground in pouring rain—from water cannons, that is!

There's got to be a better way to get around! This task took place 400 feet above the neon lights of the Vegas Strip. Players shinnied across a semicircle from one side of the hotel to the other, hanging on for dear life and releasing flags along the way.

Swinging Their Fears Away!

One hundred feet over the water, players attempting this scary stunt had to move from swing to swing. There were fifty of them. Careful, caaaaareful . . .

"Here I come! Here I come!"

Maybe it would be better to sit and grab!

The winner finished the task in less than five fearful minutes.

SPLASH DOWN!

Welcome to the *Fear Factor* water park! Oceans, lakes, and even water tanks are places where contestants faced their hydrophobia, or fear of water:

Water Sack: Players were handcuffed and sealed in sacks before being dropped into a freezing water tank, where they had to release themselves and swim to the surface. Only one player completed this task. The others, well, tanked.

Hurricane Slide: Players climbed a Plexiglas tunnel, collecting flags as water and 100-mile-per-hour winds hit them head-on.

Kid-a-Pult: On *Fear Factor*, kids slid down a zip line into a lake, swam to a barge, and then were catapulted thirty feet into the water by their parents. Cool!